Praise for UNFL.

René Koesler's integrity, determination, passions for excellence, coupled with her heart and love of nature has paved the way for her to share these DEEP and transformative leadership lessons. I couldn't put it down! She makes you want to be better with each step, and in all areas of your life!

Kathleen Ronald
Keynote Speaker
Business Consultant

While many writers use mountains as metaphors, very few have ever climbed one and even fewer have done so with the thoughtfulness and reflection that leads to true insight and learning. René Koesler is one of those few. In her new book *Unflappable: Leadership Lessons from Climbing Mountains,* René harvests stories from her years of hiking and climbing and combines these experiences with her knowledge of leadership gained from years of research and time in the classroom. The result is an engaging and accessible read, with lessons of value to all who are working to advance their own leadership skills.

Marge Connelly
Former COO of Wachovia
Securities, Barclaycard, and Convergys

If you're looking for a book that captivates, inspires, and motivates the reader to greater heights, then René Koesler's book *Unflappable: Leadership Lessons from Climbing Mountains,* is a must read. As a real-life mountain climber,

Rená becomes your trusted guide to what leadership really is and how to use it, enabling you to reach your own summits! Before stepping onto any mountain, I want Rená beside me. Hang on and enjoy the ride!

Gary Barnes
President, Gary Barnes International

Beautifully written book that puts leadership in the fascinating context of mountain climbing and brings the word unflappable into a new light. This is a book from the heart of an accomplished and self-reflective woman. Mountain climbing works so well in a context to teach us about leadership. This book is above the genre of leadership books. I only wish it were longer.

Dr. Ken Perkins
Provost Emeritus at Longwood University

UNFLAPPABLE
Leadership Lessons from Climbing Mountains

UNFLAPPABLE
Leadership Lessons from Climbing Mountains

RENÁ KOESLER

SUMMIT PRESS
Morrison, Colorado

Published by:
Summit Press
Morrison, Colorado
www.RenaKoesler.com

Rená Koesler can be reached at:
Rena@RenaKoesler.com

Paperback ISBN: 978-0-578-31596-6

Book publishing services by YellowStudios

First Edition.

Printed in the United States of America.

Dedication

It is of no surprise that I dedicate this book in honor of my Dad. He was, and continues to be, instrumental in my character and growth. Only once did I ever hear my Dad say he was proud of me. I know he was proud of me more than that one time but hearing him verbalize it carried so much more weight and value than if he said it many times over.

His life was simple, not money driven. Growing up on a farm during the Great Depression carried a special value. Hard work was what he knew and cutting corners was not his way of treating others or demonstrating responsibility. Modeling good character was what he learned and valued. It is what makes me proud to call him Dad.

I also want to dedicate this book to all the students I've had the pleasure of inspiring and leading. Campers from Girl Scout counseling days, students from the Wilderness Education Association (WEA), from the National Outdoor Leadership School (NOLS), the Wilderness Institute for Leadership Development (WILD) Outdoors Program, Longwood University, Teton Science Schools, Masterclass, and my Mastermind on the Mountain program. It is the "student" that inspires me to be better and do better. Thank you!

Lastly, this book is dedicated to the mentors that I had throughout my life. The following are the women and men that showed me the way, provided a solid example of character and leadership, and above all else, supported and guided me in my leadership growth process. Dr. Frank Lupton, Paul Petzoldt, Jim Rennie, Dr. Mildred (Mickey) Little, and Dr. Bette Harris—thank you!

Contents

Foreword

I met Rená Koesler in 2012. We were students in a writing seminar at the John C. Campbell Folk School in the mountains of North Carolina. My first impression was that Rená and I couldn't be more different.

Rená, a college professor of Outdoor Education, was spending a week at the writing seminar before heading out for a solo hike on the John Muir Trail (JMT) in California. I recently retired from a thirty-year corporate career in human resources, marketing, and communications. I was establishing myself as a freelance writer and a life coach. My idea of an outdoor adventure was sitting on the deck of a mountaintop cabin taking in the view.

Throughout the week our instructor tossed out prompts to inspire our writing. Rená insisted that she wasn't a writer. Her intention was to pump up her journaling muscles so that she could record insights and experiences while on the JMT.

I remember that her essays were personal, humorous, and filled with sensory delights. Even more than her writing, I remember how she encouraged me and others in the class with her enthusiastic response to our unpolished words.

One evening, after class, I invited Rená and our instructor to have dinner with me and the friend with whom I was staying. Wine, good food and musings about the creative process shaped our conversation. As we grew more comfortable with each other we took turns talking about the challenges of relationships and the aspirations for the next phases of our lives.

In hindsight I would use the word "unflappable" to describe Rená's give and take that evening. She sat calmly as a witness to our heartbreak; she encouraged each of us to step into our dreams. When she told her stories she spoke with candor and courage. She trusted us enough to reveal setbacks and to describe the unknown horizons she faced as a hiker, as a teacher, and as a woman.

By the end of the week I realized that my first impression of Rená hadn't given either one of us enough credit. She and I had much more in common than I could have imagined. Although we had different life experiences, we shared a commitment to learning and leading.

I waved farewell to my new friend as she pulled out of the Folk School parking lot. I envied her as she headed West in her Subaru Outback loaded with provisions for her hiking adventure.

Rená and I have kept in touch since the writing seminar that forged our friendship. She was one of the first people I contacted when, in 2015, I decided to hike the Grand Canyon

"You can do this!" she said. Her confidence far outweighed mine. Rená hiked into and out of the Grand Canyon several times. She gave me some tips, suggested a few books, and cheered from afar as I trained for this adventure.

I was wise enough to book this Grand Canyon expedition with skilled hikers. The morning of our descent into the canyon we hiked for a couple of hours when I needed to take off my pack and sit down. My clumsy gait and a too heavy of a backpack wrenched my back muscles.

I flapped! In tears I blamed myself for not training enough, and for packing too much stuff. When I calmed down, I said "Yes" to my companions' offer to carry my pack. They helped me see that refusing their help would worsen my injury. Being stubborn would also put them at risk if we got stranded on the path because I was unable to carry myself and my pack to the bottom of the canyon.

Before Rená moved to Colorado in 2018, a friend and I traveled from Maryland to Virginia for a daylong hike with her in Shenandoah National Park. I was still a slow and sometimes flappable hiker, sliding down steep descents on my butt and huffing up steep inclines, certain I was going to die. My other friend, who had been on the Grand Canyon hike, ignored my flapping. She meandered with me, taking photos, studying plants.

Rená kept a steady pace, never losing sight of us slower hikers. We stopped for water, and a snack at each rest point. As we sipped and munched, we shared thoughts about what we had seen and what insights were arising.

One of the best parts of a long hike is finding a place to toast the experience with a beer and to restore calories burned with a good meal. After this hike in the Shenandoah Mountains, Rená suggested that we go to a local brew pub for an early dinner. The place was hopping with hikers and visitors.

Over the din of music and conversation we heard voices yell, "Dr. Koesler!" A group of Rená's former students from Longwood University circled her with hugs.

Standing on the sideline I listened as these young people told Rená about their latest adventures. Each of them, in saying goodbye, reminded her how much they missed her and how happy they were to see her again. Their reaction to Rená showed me that her unflappable spirit was one of the greatest gifts she passed on to her students.

Today, Rená would still say that she is not a writer. This may be the only thing about where we disagree. She has now published two books, both of which use simple language and real-life stories to inspire leaders of all sorts to claim their authority.

In *Unflappable,* Rená demonstrates who she is as a friend and as a leader – an influencer, a caregiver, a cheerleader, and a risk taker. She radiates authority and integrity; she exudes integrity and joy.

In her books, on her Mastermind on the Mountain program hikes, and Masterclasses, Rená offers tips for how to apply lessons she experienced in climbing mountains, leading teams, and pursuing goals. She admits mistakes she has made along the way. She reveals how her love of the outdoors strengthens her body, sharpens her mind, and nurtures her spirit.

Rená embodies the word unflappable. She does this by living as a learner, leading as a teacher. I can hear her telling us all, when we may doubt our own unflappable spirit, "You can do this!"

Linda Mastro
Living Pilgrimage: Spiritual Guidance for Daily Living

Acknowledgements

In the order of book contributions, I first want to thank Dr. Dennis Propst for his willingness to take the first early read of my book. As my PhD advisor and chief editor of my doctoral dissertation, he was a very logical choice. More than twenty-five years later, he was gracious enough to provide the time and insightful feedback. His comments helped shape the tone and direction of the book.

My dear friend Linda Mastro comes next. I was so honored she was willing to write the foreword for my book as I hold her and her writing in high esteem. I'm so glad her name is represented in my book as our mutual writing journeys and friendship began in a writing workshop.

The four people I asked to write a testimony for me all said yes. Each of them represent components of character and leadership that I strongly admire and are worthy of recognition. Kathleen Ronald for her heart, consistency, and the authentic value she brings to others through coaching and speaking. Dr. Ken Perkins for his leadership and loyalty to me and Longwood University.

Marge Connelly for her leadership as modeled to and for women. Her contributions in business and education have not gone unnoticed. Gary Barnes for his business coaching and advice. He thrives on watching others succeed, including me.

I want to applaud Jennifer Doss for her creativity, patience, and availability as we worked on the book cover.

She has been a dream to work with on this book and other projects.

I want to thank and recognize my life partner, Eva. She is my greatest cheerleader. Not only was she an armchair editor, but she also consistently believed in me and supported my purpose for writing the book throughout the many phases.

To my first editor, Kathy Brown, thank you! I appreciated her words of encouragement, her flexibility, and the ease in working together. To my second editor, Veronica Yager at YellowStudios, thank you. I have most valued her expertise in packaging and designing the final stages of the book.

Introduction

WE ALL HAVE INFLUENCES AND INFLUENCERS WHO SHAPE OUR LIVES. I've lived long enough to see, experience, and learn from the events and people in my life to share my views of leadership. Perhaps I could have written something a year ago, five years ago, or when I experienced my greatest defining moment in leadership several years ago. But I chose to write this book now when the desire is right in front of me. I am inspired and don't want to get somewhere in the future and look back saying, "I shoulda, coulda, woulda" and regret never doing it.

On average, there are four to five leadership books published daily. Here is one more. No leadership book has all the insights and answers. What could I possibly say about leadership that has not already been written about, mused over or experienced? The stories I share shaped my continuous insights into leadership, beginning with my first "aha" moment in leading: the value of being unflappable, particularly in times of uncertainty.

There are leaders who did not have the mentors and role models I had, or climbed mountains on their way to leadership, or experienced tragedy along the way. However, these experiences gave me insight and examples to follow, triggered my desire to learn and grow, and the judgment necessary to strengthen my leadership.

Mentoring was most significant, particularly for women.

I followed leaders, witnessed leaders lead, attended leadership seminars, held leadership positions, and taught leadership. I've read at least a zillion written works about leadership for over 40 years. Even my doctoral dissertation was entitled: *Factors Influencing Leadership Development in Wilderness Education*. I found that goal attainment, feedback, and mentoring have a direct impact on one's self-efficacy (e.g., the perception of one's ability to perform a task). The greater the self-efficacy found through experience, performance attainment, mentoring, and feedback, the greater the correlation found in leadership confidence and success. Mentoring was found to be most significant, particularly for women, in the process of continued development as a leader. This research statistic alone validated my personal experience and the invaluable growth I gained from having mentors in my development as a leader.

All this education does not make me a leadership expert, rather it is the length of time invested in leadership. It is what I've learned from leading and observing behaviors. I relied heavily on my mentors and leaders to model leadership for me. I reflected on experiences to gain the judgment necessary to improve on the next leadership opportunity. And I also invested in those who were in my group or on my team. I wanted and needed to know who they were, what they wanted, and why they were a part of the experience.

Beyond the seminars I attended, articles I read, and roles I played, my greatest growth was from leading, following, and observing others in my own pursuit of climbing mountains. My favorite class to teach at Longwood University was *Leadership Development Through Wilderness Pursuits*. For thirty years, I provided adventure experiences (rock climbing and backpacking trips) where the students utilized direct experiences to develop leadership by way of their actions and decisions.

Using lessons and insights gained from years of putting one foot in front of the other revealed elements of what influenced me as well as what I could do to influence others. Characteristics such as unselfishness, consistency, teamwork, self-awareness, willingness to take risks, sound judgment, good character, and being UNFLAPPABLE directed me toward the factors necessary in leading.

Leadership is influence, nothing more and nothing less.

John Maxwell is considered the number one leadership authority in America. He has written over seventy books on leadership. I support his definition of leadership as: "leadership is influence, nothing more and nothing less." People commonly recognize titles and positions when they identify someone as a leader. Titles may initially mean something, but if the title is not supported by influence, then leadership is in name only, not in action.

Some of the greatest influencers in my life were those I followed on outdoor adventures. I quickly realized that the authenticity of the outdoor environment enabled me to see a leader as trustworthy and ethical without airs or façades. I learned early on not to be fooled or enticed by a leader's title, the clothes they wear, their gender, or their credentials.

Leadership was more authentically demonstrated due to the extended amount of time spent in the wilderness. It is hard to be someone you are not in the wilderness, surrounded by daily uncertainties and the spontaneous adventures experienced along the way. Decision making and leadership is readily practiced and applied.

Know what you know and know what you don't know.

I shared this quote with college students throughout my career as an Outdoor Education Professor. This quote resonated far beyond the classes I taught and into students' personal lives. It reflects a leader's ability to admit they don't know the correct answer rather than boasting or fabricating one. Outcomes in actions and decisions in the outdoor environment are real with little room for error. As a climber and outdoor leader, bluffing through an answer had serious and life-altering consequences to the follower such as "I *think* this is the right knot to tie, or I *think* this is the way to go, or I *think* this is the right equipment to use." Recognizing what you know and what you don't know breeds mutual trust between the leader and the participants and reflects good character.

No one is born with character or should I say character-based leadership. It is earned through successes and mistakes, blunders, and a lot of reflection on how to improve and BE a person of character. The development of character is formed from one's genetics, biases, desires, character traits, intuition, emotions, and social norms. Character-based leadership can't be accomplished without some thoughtful introspection from the mistakes we've made, and the street smarts gained from life experiences.

Influence without character is
dead-end leadership.

My Dad was a man of character. He didn't start that way but by the time he got to me, the youngest in the family, all I saw was a halo over his head. Well, not really, especially when I was disciplined or unable to get what I wanted. He was trustworthy, showed up, followed through, was a man of his word, very consistent in actions and words, and humble in demeanor. Through his simple but resonating gems of wisdom, he continued to impact the character legacy he bestowed on me. My siblings and I affectionately repeat these gems of wisdom in honor and love of who he represented in our lives. I talk more about my Dad in Chapter One but for now, he warrants recognition as the first role model and influencer in my life.

Leadership begins with YOU.

Everyone has leadership potential and has every right and desire to identify themselves as a leader. Whether you are a parent, a mountain climber, a teacher, a grocery clerk, or the CEO of Amazon, you have influence. The power of influence can result in good or bad outcomes. However, *influence without character is dead-end leadership.* Who do you trust, honor, and respect? Character-based leadership recognizes the person who models integrity, emotional intelligence, consistency, trustworthiness, and openness. These qualities drive influence and support character-based leadership.

The most challenging component of leadership is learning to lead yourself. This component is paramount to leading others. It requires knowing yourself, your abilities, your responses, your intentions, your commitments, your consistencies, and the value you bring to others. Once you can lead yourself, leadership requires less effort with greater impact.

The process of leading myself began with the decision to go to college. I initially went to college because my friends were going. But once I climbed my first mountain, the desire to influence others was revealed. It's hard to silence a passion. I couldn't wait to share what I experienced with others. It was as if I was saying "I want you to experience this too."

Nothing stopped my pursuit of learning more and leading myself. I searched for continued personal growth as I followed my driven desire. I made the decisions and changes necessary to learn more about myself and to make a difference. This desire stretched my abilities and furthered my comprehension of what "potential" really meant.

Although I didn't know it at the time, I busted out of my perceived family expectations and away from what my friends were doing in order to follow my own drumbeat. My independent nature helped in this process as I pursued ideas and goals that were uniquely different from those in my social circle. I didn't know anyone with an adventurous spirit and certainly didn't know anyone who climbed mountains.

I traveled alone to parts of the world where many, especially women, would not even consider. But I wanted to be stretched and discover my own resourcefulness and decision-making abilities in unknown environments. My domestic and international solo excursions, often in the pursuit of climbing a mountain, gave me the opportunity to learn about myself, other cultures, and people I met along the way. These challenging experiences and chance encounters became the hallmark of my growth in leadership and influence.

Since then, I have climbed many mountains around the world and have summitted many more due to repeated climbs of the same mountain. I've climbed little mountains, big mountains, technical mountains, walk up mountains, and mountains requiring mountaineering expertise. I found that I gained more than I ever anticipated from the challenge it requires to climb. IF I continue to put one foot in the front of the other, I will reach more and discover more than I could have previously imagined.

What Will You Find Inside?

I've been keeping diaries, logbooks, and journals since fifth grade. As I unpacked and read my journals to find the stories I share in this book, I am quickly reminded of the fragility and strength found in leadership. My journal accounts brought me immediately back to the scene, the environment, the emotions, and the events that unfolded during those experiences. Leadership is dynamic. However, remaining unflappable during the most uncertain times helped me gain the consistency and confidence as a leader.

Leadership Development is in the Climb. The stories are a selection of collected adventures which include a mixture of what I learned from successes and what I learned from failures in climbing mountains. Although I never climbed Mt. Everest, I climbed my own Everest's that were profoundly instrumental in my leadership growth.

The Value of Vulnerability. I share the ups and downs, the good and bad, and the yin and yang of the stories. Sometimes we learn less from successes or perhaps take for granted the successes we euphorically achieve. I have learned to humble myself in the successes of reaching summits and the courage to be vulnerable in my failures. It is in this spirit of openness that will help you formulate insights from what you read.

The Value of Stories in Leadership Development. My intention in writing this book is to invite you to ask more questions, compare the concepts I present to your own assertions of leadership, and to nod your head in agreement or shake your head in disagreement. My greatest leadership lessons were discovered in climbing mountains. I hope the stories I share garner insight that add to your library of what leadership is or can be for you.

1

MY FIRST INFLUENCER

My Dad was born in 1910. People born then are no longer living, so my accounts of him are based on memories kept alive in our family. I fondly use his birth year, 1910, to reference an event or a moment a long time ago.

He was so proud of his farm boy childhood, walking in the snow for miles to school, working on the farm, riding tractors, bailing hay, milking the cows, and stacking wood. He just loved physical labor. He was even proud of his farmer's tan.

His skin just above the bicep was stark white but everything below was dark brown signifying the hours spent in the hot sun plowing the fields. He was especially proud of the strength of his hand grip, even at 93. His big farmer hands would give a good grip with anyone, man or woman, and expressed the contract it held between people. My Dad was a quiet and "unflappable" man when I was growing up. He was a man of few words and his actions spoke volumes.

The honor of his word was found in a solid handshake.

Isn't that how it is supposed to be where your actions speak louder than your words? But, as he grew in his senior and twilight years, he began to open up more, share his stories and be more talkative, particularly around his church social group. Everyone was a "great guy." I rarely, if ever, heard him speak negatively about someone else.

He married young and had a rough beginning. Although he had two children from his first marriage, he was restless and headed west, leaving his relatively new family behind. It took exploring on his own and his parents failing health to bring him back to the midwest to confront the life he escaped. But it didn't end there as he met my mother. However their rocky marriage resulted in divorce. Their short union produced four children, including me. Upon their divorce, we were all placed in an orphanage located in northern Illinois.

After two and a half years of my parents figuring out their own lives, we finally left the orphanage. My Dad had remarried and the children were divided between my parents. My two oldest siblings went with my mother and my brother, closest in age to me, and I lived with my father. Over time, all of us ended up living with my father.

I was the youngest of the bunch with little memory of living at the orphanage. I was one and half years old when we went to the orphanage and four when we left and moved in with my father and his new wife.

My new home was in the country, about a mile and a half from the nearest little town. I often sat between two lilac bushes on the hill just off the driveway near the garage. I nibbled on grass while looking out over the creek and woods in the distance. Perhaps this was the start of my interest in wild edibles and my desire to seek adventure in wild and natural places.

Come late spring and early summer, my stepmother and I walked the country road to pick wild asparagus, filling the paper grocery bags every day. Our family home had cherry trees just outside our back door and a huge oak tree in our back yard. What is it about big trees that entice children to climb them?

I was accustomed to seeing garter snakes, frogs, rabbits, mice, and a collection of creepy crawly things. Little did I know at the time, these fond memories and early experiences set the stage to follow a career involving nature and the great outdoors.

My Dad was the head of the household. It was evident in every way. When he spoke, we listened. There was never a spanking, a slap, or any kind of physical punishment. But what is it about a Dad raising his voice that makes children stand still or run? Don't be late, turn off the lights when you are not in the room, don't skip school, and work hard and save money for a rainy day were "mantras" we consistently heard from Dad.

I fondly recall our designated places at the table. My parents sat at each end and I sat to the right of Dad at the long end of the table. My brother sat across from me to my Dad's left side. We began our meal with a memorized simple prayer, "Dear Lord, thank you for this food and this day and bless our home, In Jesus' name we ask, Amen."

Dad often shared his food with us at the table even though he was the one who worked all day. It wasn't that we didn't have enough food. I think it was his upbringing and growing up in the Depression era, not to mention that I ate faster than everyone else, prompting him to cut a little piece of meat and place it on my plate. I didn't realize the value of sharing from this memory until I became a leader.

I was not an early riser in high school and college, but as I matured, I realized I really liked mornings. Given the influence of Dad's farm boy background coupled with my first wilderness instructor's influence, I saw the leadership significance of getting up in the morning and the value it models for others.

No matter how old I became he was still my Dad and the one I went to for advice. His comments and phrases were always simple.

"You can do anything you put your mind to…"

"Everybody's different…" and

"You got through it, didn't you?"

He never committed an answer to the common question a child often asks a parent; "What should I do, Dad?" He found the words that essentially said:

"You'll figure it out" or

"Do what you want to do."

He trusted me enough to explore my own path as he gave me the freedom and independence to pursue my interests.

The endearing memories and lessons learned from Dad continue to remind me of the leadership values he modeled; serving others first, don't be late, work hard, tell the truth, trust in others, and demonstrate a life of character in word and deed. It is never too late to develop character.

Dad visiting us at St. Vincent's Orphanage

Dad's 90th Birthday Party

Reflective Questions

1. Who in your life do you believe has had great influence on who you are and what you have become?

2. What is it about them that separates them from other people in your life?

3. How important do you believe character is in your ability to lead?

2

WHEN IT STARTED

The decisions we make are most often based on our values; our personal judgments of what is important to us and what matters most to us. Sometimes it takes pushing away from the familiar to discern what we really do value. But sometimes we don't know what we value until an event or experience triggers an emotional response that takes us completely by surprise.

In 1973, at the age of 17, I wasn't sure what I valued. Yes, I valued my family, but I really valued my friends. Although I couldn't put my finger on it at the time, I really valued freedom and independence; the chance to sneak out of the house, have my own car, and to be with my friends on weekend shenanigans. I couldn't wait to get behind the wheel and go somewhere. I would drive all over town to pick up my friends in my 1970 gold Chevy Nova. I valued what my friends valued and that worked for me until I failed out of college.

The decisions we make are directly related to the values we hold.

I didn't intend to go to college. Furthering my education beyond high school, wasn't something sought after in my family. My Dad only graduated from the eighth grade so his thought about education was second to hard work. Going to college was simply not something I thought I would be doing until the arrival of my senior year in high school. Many of my friends were going to college and I wasn't going to stay home and work in a factory. I enrolled in college because my friends were going to college and going to THAT college. I thought it was a "cool" idea but only because there was freedom to be on my own.

My freshman year was a blast. Yes, I partied, skipped classes, made a ton of new friends, and learned so much about life beyond my small town. My less than good grades were an indication of what I valued most – my friends and fun. Given that I valued my social life more than my academic life, I was suspended a year from college due to my poor grades. I was devastated and spent the year working in a smoke detector factory, vowing that I would do what it took to get back to school. My values were shifting. There is always growth in learning from failures.

When the following summer came, I enrolled in summer school classes and I received all A's for the summer. The A's were enough to get me back in college full-time. My values shifted again. For me to continue in school, I had to make good grades. My academic life now became my value since it was directly tied to ensuring I would stay in college, get a degree, and still be with my friends.

I majored in Parks and Recreation Administration. The Recreation Department was offering a program the following academic year that included a semester-long opportunity to travel around the country, spending a month in the Wyoming mountains, visiting outdoor and environmental centers and obtain a semester's worth of grades in the process.

It simply sounded too good to be true. No desks to sit in, no papers to write, no tests to take – all experiential. So I signed up for this program. Oh, how I was hoping to be selected.

While anticipating the news, I received a letter from Dr. Frank Lupton, the professor and leader of the wilderness program, saying I was first on the waiting list. Oh goodness, how could this be? However, a week later I got a phone call saying someone dropped out. If I was still interested, I could now go on the program. I was ecstatic. I recall running down my dorm hallway jumping and screaming the great news. Values continued shifting.

The name of the program was Environmental Conservation Outdoor Education Expedition (ECOEE). I enjoyed the outdoors which was inspired from growing up in the country and from my former Girl Scout days. But this was new and certainly out of my comfort zone. The night before leaving on a restored school bus to drive west with a group of strangers, I cried.

I was scared. I wasn't sure what I was getting myself into as I was embarking on a semester-long program with a group of people I didn't know. I was leaving the comforts of my friends and the experiences I would not be able to share. But I was considering my value of freedom to continue exploring what and who I was, even if it took sacrificing a few memories with my friends along the way. I was beginning to realize that…

There is little growth and discovery in the comfort zone.

It's awkward meeting people for the first time, especially at a young age. What they say, how they say it, who talks more, who seems nice, and who you might want to stay away from were thoughts running through my mind. They are called first impressions. Everyone makes a first impression and everyone else is gathering their impression of you and others.

The fits and starts in getting to know people not in my social circle was uncomfortable. It wasn't until our backpacks were packed and carried down the trail did the authentic side of people begin to surface. First impressions are important at first, but if taken without openness beyond that initial impression, you may be out of a potential friend.

Paul Petzoldt, the first mountain man and wilderness leader I had ever met, was going to be our instructor for our wilderness leadership course in Wyoming. He is the founder of the National Outdoor Leadership School (NOLS) and the founder of the Wilderness Education Association (WEA), both renowned wilderness education programs with the main focus on leadership development.

He was a big, tall man with a booming voice, hairy eyebrows, and wore a size 14 boot. Those characteristics alone were intimidating, but I saw the look in his eyes and the underlying softness and care he emulated. As the course began, we learned how to build a fire, where to pitch a tent, how to cook a healthy and decent meal, how to dress comfortably for any type of weather, and how to take care of the environment as we traveled.

Since this was a leadership course, there were specific lessons on leadership and questions about what was gained from each day's experience. The leadership characteristic that Paul placed at the top of the list was unselfishness. Although skills, knowledge, and experience along with many other characteristics were on the list, Paul taught us that unselfishness reminded us to put others first. Paul became my mentor and role model as I witnessed his ease, comfort and unflappable disposition in challenging and uncertain situations.

After three weeks in the wilderness, we moved into the technical skills of rappelling and rock climbing. Wearing a wool hat, wool long underwear, wool socks, and army surplus wool pants was common outdoor clothing in 1977.

I experienced my first rappel in the Wind River Mountains in Wyoming on September 30th. Although it was scary going over the edge for the first time it was also really fun. We learned about rope handling, how to tie our seat harnesses, and how to arrange our six aluminum carabiners in such a way so when feeding the rope through them on a rappel, it created the necessary friction to slow and guide our decent.

October 1st became a chance for most of us to experience our first technical rock climb up the 12,000-plus feet of a mountain called Petroleum Peak. At this stage of the expedition, I wanted to experience everything this program and place could offer. Since the assistant instructor took a group up the mountain in the early morning, we didn't leave our base camp until mid-afternoon.

By the time we reached the base of the mountain to begin climbing, the sun was getting lower in the western sky. The length of the climb involved three rope lengths (approximately 150 ft.) known as pitches to the top. Out of four students, I was last in line. By the time I reached the top it was nearly dark. What an experience! According to my journal, I used every part of my body in reaching the top. Climbing in steel-shank mountaineering boots without a helmet was an acceptable climbing norm and a commonly used practice at the time. This only added to the epic experience.

As we reached the base of the mountain after our rappel, it was completely dark and well into the evening hours. With one flashlight among us, our instructor got us across the boulder fields, through the willows, and into our campsite safely at 10,800 feet in elevation. It was 11:30 pm and 16 degrees on a Saturday night.

The ability to face the fear, accept the challenge, believe in my own abilities, trust the other team members to stay the course, and a full reliance on our leader unearthed a desire I never remotely encountered before. The emotional transformation I was experiencing was dramatic and fostered an enormous shift in my values. I awoke the next morning and said,

...this is what I want to do for the rest of my life!

Call it a dream, a desire, or a light bulb. This transformative experience unleashed my calling, shaped my values, and became the beacon to my future decisions. There was no stopping my desire to become a leader and inspire others to step out, do something new, get out of the comfort zone, take risks, and continue growing.

The lighting of my spiritual compass illuminated my direction. Recognizing the novelty and power found in this awakening, gave rise to my desire to lead others into the wild outdoors. Ultimately, it was and is my spiritual faith in God that gives me strength, courage, and the desire to reach the symbolic summits in my own life.

1977 ECOEE Group with
Doc Frank Lupton and Paul Petzoldt

The first day of backpacking on ECOEE

My first rappell

Petroleum Peak
My first leadership climbing experience

Reflective Questions

1. Is there a moment in time when you recognized that there was a considerable shift in your values?

2. How did those values impact the decision you made and the direction you took in your life?

3. Have you encountered a transformational experience that ignited your passion and desire? Do you still have the passion and desire?

4. What area in your life are you choosing to shift today?

3

UNFLAPPABLE
LEADERSHIP

I was now out of college and dreaming about my desire to return to Wyoming. Magical things happened to my spirit. Like a child who had their first taste of ice cream, there is no dissolving that taste. I was offered my first full-time job from my college internship at the Rockford, Illinois YMCA. Although I enjoyed the job, the taste of that ice cream never left my palate. After 18 months, the tasty urge became overwhelming. I left my job in 1980, drove across the country to Driggs, Idaho to answer the call to my next unknown adventure.

There was $200 in my savings account, and I spent the bulk of it on a new pair of cross-country skis and boots when I arrived. Having skis helped me merge into the winter outdoor culture, particularly since the only person I knew was Paul Petzoldt.

Paul invited me to come out to his lodge in Alta, Wyoming (just outside of Driggs, Idaho). I got a job at the nearby Targhee ski resort for the winter and quickly caught on to the winter social activities. Like Dad, I too took the opportunity to explore, learn, and be free of expectations.

Living in the area and being around Paul had its advantages. As spring approached, Paul offered me the opportunity to instruct summer wilderness courses in the Tetons and Wind River Range. As scary as it felt, I accepted the challenge. I knew this was my next step and would dramatically expand my circle of comfort. By now, I had taken two Wilderness Education Association (WEA) courses with Paul as my instructor. He had become my mentor and role model and I wanted to capitalize on all that I could from his expertise and knowledge.

Now here I was face to face with moving from participant to leader and teaching alongside Paul. I was empowered by his confidence in me as he said I was ready to lead. Two things he said to me starting out:

"Speak with confidence and talk from your diaphragm (core) versus your voice box."

"Don't let your nose peel from sun exposure."

The 1981 all-women's WEA course was the first and only course of its type since the birth of the WEA in 1977. It wasn't an authentic all-women's course since Paul was the lead instructor. I was only 25 years old and a no-name, but the course filled quickly because of Paul Petzoldt's name and reputation. Given that there were no other female instructors at the time, Paul had to be the other instructor to pull this course off. He was a huge support for women in leadership and offering this course spoke volumes to his vision for growth in female outdoor leaders.

Even though I had initial experience as a WEA Instructor in the Tetons just prior to the women's course, I was nervous and quite intimidated by the age, experience, and credentials of the women in this course. Many of the women were twice my age, and many of them with PhDs in Outdoor Education. Why in the world would they listen to or follow someone half their age and experience?

On the first day of the course in the Wind River Mountains, I taught a class on packing a backpack. As I began to teach, I asked the group of women, "Would you all mind sitting? This class will take some time and sitting would be more comfortable for you." Actually, having them sit was more comfortable for me. But they immediately sat and I felt my comfort level rise and my confidence in leading increase. They were willing to adhere to my request and I didn't compromise my own level of comfort. It sounds elementary but at that time, everything was an experiment as I continued to find my voice and style in teaching and leading. Following through with my voice was key to my leadership development.

About two weeks into the expedition, Paul asked me to lead a group of women up Petroleum Peak, where I had my first transformative climbing experience. Although I climbed it twice before, I was now in a position of leadership where I needed to tap into my previous experience and knowledge of the peak. Four women stayed behind with Paul at basecamp and the remaining eight women followed me as we hiked through a boulder field toward the base of the peak. Upon arrival at the base and before the women tied their harnesses in preparation for the climb, the weather from the west looked ominous. The clouds were changing from a white to a much darker shade of gray. I was thinking to myself:

- What am I going to do?

- What is the weather going to do?

- Would we be able to make it to the top and down before the storm strikes?

- How disappointed would the group be if we didn't make it to the top?

- What's the best decision given the group, the weather, and the unknown?

We waited to evaluate the weather patterns from the western sky. Not much change. The women were patient and waited for a call from me…up or down? Either Paul told them not to say anything to me or they were allowing me to internally struggle through the process of making a good judgment decision.

I recall Dr. Margaret Miller, a professor from California say to me, "You are unflappable." I had never heard the term before. Eventually I learned that the word unflappable is a complimentary characteristic for someone who stays the course under times of uncertainty in a calm manner.

After watching, discerning, and navigating my surroundings for 45 minutes, I decided that we should head back to base camp. By the time we returned, it was nearly dark, and Paul was obviously relieved that we returned safely. In the end, it never fully rained, only sprinkled. I wasn't disappointed and neither were the group members.

We collectively recognized the value in good judgment and embraced the leadership experience gained.

As a young leader, this was a profound leadership experience for me. The older, wiser, and more experienced women on the course never took the leadership away from me. For the first time, I recognized the value in the journey, not in reaching a goal or the destination.

Growth is not always gained from reaching the top.

I grew in leaps and bounds on that course because of the freedom to lead, the ability to step out and experiment with my voice and style and to be supported and trusted by Paul and the participants on the course.

WEA shakedown trip in Teton Canyon
with Paul Petzoldt

Making tang-flavored snow cones
on the All-Women's Group Trip

Boulder Field with All-Women's Group

All-Women's Group with Paul Petzoldt

Reflective Questions

1. Do you have a mentor in your life that will support, encourage, and challenge you to grow? What value does your mentor(s) bring to you?

2. What was your first "aha" moment in leading? What did it teach you?

3. When you found your voice, did it make a difference in your leadership ability and style?

4. What other areas in your life or business would you like to illuminate your voice?

4

WIND RIVER
MOUNTAINS

After my "gap" time in Wyoming, I decided to head to Texas for graduate school in 1982. I never thought I would be living in Texas, but one of the professors in the WEA women's course invited me to consider graduate school at Texas A&M University. Knowing a highly respected Outdoor Education professor had its perks. Dr. Mickey Little became my mentor and was very influential in securing a job for me working for the Outdoor Program in the student union. Her investment in my growth played a significant role in my leadership development.

While working for the Outdoor Program, I wanted to use the teaching and leadership skills I acquired from the WEA to give students the power of the wilderness experience I had encountered. So, I created and started the Wilderness Institute for Leadership Development (WILD) outdoors program. The WEA curriculum stretched out over a year in the WILD outdoors program involving canoeing, backpacking, and team-building adventures culminating in a four-week summer expedition to the Wind River Mountains in Wyoming.

Camille, a professor at Texas A&M, and I were the lead female instructors for this 12-participant wilderness course. After rationing our food and packing our packs, we loaded (2) 15-passenger vehicles and drove 13 hours across Texas, on through New Mexico, Colorado, and into Wyoming. It was the first time these east Texas-born students had seen mountains.

We prepared the students throughout the semester to start a fire, pitch a tent, cook a meal, protect the environment, and travel as a group. They were ready to begin using these skills in a new environment over an extended period of time.

We arrived at Dickinson Park, located on the east side of the Wind River Mountains. We backpacked twenty plus miles and conducted leadership classes over multiple days to arrive at Baptiste Lake along the Continental Divide. We found ourselves at the foot of Petroleum Peak once again. The scenery was beautiful, the fishing outstanding, and the wildflowers were in full bloom in mid-July. The memories of this area always warmed my soul.

We were not the only group camped at Baptiste Lake, however. Paul Petzoldt was leading another expedition group camped on the north side of the lake. There were experienced climbers in his course who wanted to climb a couloir (a steep narrow ice crusted snow passage in the side of a mountain) to the west of us along the Continental Divide. With Paul's permission, two females and one male set out with a rope, ice axes, and climbing hardware to climb the glacier-like snow slope to the top of the Continental Divide.

At the time, I did not know that Paul kept an eye on them through binoculars from his basecamp. He saw they made it to the top, but as the morning extended into early afternoon and temperatures warmed, so did the snow.

As Paul watched them climb down the slope, he saw that one of them had fallen. Since the climbers were all tied together by the climbing rope, none of their attempts to self-arrest (digging the pick of the ice axe into the snow to halt a fall) with their ice axes stopped them in the soft snow. They all tumbled down the steep slope, pulling each other from the tension in the rope and stopping on the edge of a boulder field at the bottom of the couloir.

Paul sent runners from his camp to ours on the south side of the lake. We pulled together four runners from our group, including me. We packed food, a first aid kit, shelter, and headed to the base of the couloir. It took us about 45 minutes to get to them.

All three climbers were conscious but shaken up. Two were injured. The male had a head contusion, and one of the females had dislocated her elbow and suffered a puncture wound on the inside of her leg from the point of her ice axe. The other female was shaken but not physically injured.

Paul arrived an hour later. We were most concerned about the male, because of his head injury. We also knew the muscles around the female's dislocation would physiologically tighten to protect the injury making it difficult for her elbow to be placed back into its proper socket. Satellite communication devices were uncommon in 1982. Therefore, questions on how to evacuate them were:

- Do we send participants out to call for a helicopter?

- Do we send participants to the horse outfitters ranch to bring horses back for the injured to ride out by horseback?

- Would riding horseback cause more damage to the head injury?

- How critical is time given the injuries and the method of transportation?

This was not Paul's first rodeo, so to speak. He had many years of mountaineering experience around the globe and led many expeditions, including evacuations. Two of the three climbers warranted an evacuation. Paul's judgment was to "wait and see" as we monitored the injured students.

We checked the young man's vitals every 15 minutes through the night and into the next morning. Considering that his signs and symptoms were stable, the decision was made to bring horses in to ride out by horseback. There was no place for panic, rushing, or heroism in demonstrating leadership to others. There was confidence gained in the waiting, and Paul's unflappable demeanor contributed to the ease surrounding the event.

Trusting your judgment gives insight into a decision's timeliness.

In hindsight, there would have been less mishap if they had not roped up in the soft snow. Leaving earlier in the morning would have ensured the couloir remained solid throughout the climb.

I had no insight into the dynamics among the students. Some of the scenarios below may give a layer of understanding to the event:

- Did the male climber assume the role as leader, or was he naturally given the lead role by the females?

- Did they have the skills and knowledge to have embarked on the climbing experience?

- Did they have the necessary judgment to travel on snow and ice in warm conditions?

- Did all three climbers have the mountaineering experience to discern the advantages and disadvantages of everyone being connected by a rope?

There is value in being a spectator, even in a leadership role. Watching how the scenario unfolded and observing the calm and wait attitude Paul demonstrated was worth every piece of judgment gained. His unflappable nature settled the others' spirits and set the tone for making a mindful decision.

Baptiste Lake along the Continental Divide

Paul Petzoldt

Reflective Questions

1. Who in your life would you characterize as unflappable?

2. Identify a time when watching and observing was more valuable in your growth then acting and doing?

3. How challenging is it for you to wait to make a decision?

4. What do you need to wait for to make a good judgment decision?

5

PICO DE ORIZABA

In 1994, I just completed my Ph.D. from Michigan State University. I decided to celebrate by climbing Pico de Orizaba, the highest peak in Mexico and the third highest in North America. When I lived in Texas, traveling to Mexico was not far as we simply took buses from the Texas border to Mexico City. From there, it was only 1.5 hours to Amecameca, the base town to climb Popocatapetl, a peak I climbed in 1984. But now I lived and worked at Longwood College in Virginia.

It took a plane ride to Mexico City, a few bus transfers to get to Puebla, and another bus ride to Tlachichuca. My five comrades and I from various parts of the country (Ian, Barb, Melanie, Eric, and Jason) arrived in Mexico City in December 1994. We stayed in Puebla two nights at 8,500 feet and then a bus ride up to the Piedre Grande Huts at 14,000 feet. Pico de Orizaba stood at 18,491 feet, and the altitude of the hut system seemed like we were nearly there.

The hut was filling up with other climbers from around the world, but we found enough bunk space to be together. We organized our gear, adjusted the crampons to our boots in preparation for the next morning, and wandered about the hut looking up at Pico de Orizaba. I initially felt okay, but increasingly felt awful with a headache and upset stomach.

As dinner time approached, the food smells from the other climber's cooking were overwhelming and caused me to throw up a few times. I finally took a Diamox (a diuretic pill used to treat or prevent altitude sickness). After resting and sleeping, I felt better. I should have taken the Diamox a few days earlier. Experience does not always lead to good judgment.

We awakened at 1:00 am, ate breakfast, and began our climb by 2:00 am. I didn't feel well, but my stubbornness moved me up the mountain. We climbed over half of the ascent in the dark, partly on rocks and then on glacier. After sunrise, my crampon popped off my boot, and I dropped my ice axe on the glacier. I recall watching it slide down the 40-degree slope as it miraculously stopped about 20 feet below me.

Ian came to my rescue, retrieving the ice axe and helped me put the crampon bail back on my boot. One part of me said, "this is not good," and another part of me said, "keep it going." Regardless of feeling tired and nauseous, I summitted at 9:00 a.m.

After a few photos, a snack, and more water, we headed back down. I felt weak, and experienced cloudy vision. I had altitude sickness. I knew it, I was conscious of it, and I really tried to focus on each step on the glacier. I knew I was in a precarious situation. We approached our last ice field and halfway down my crampon popped off again. I couldn't be on the blue ice without a crampon.

I started sliding, caught myself with my other crampon, and worked my way up to a standing position. I finally had no option but to ask for help as I knew I was in a dangerous situation. Melanie came to my rescue, but my position made it very tenuous and risky for both of us. I had to slip and slide down the slope until I got to the rocks. I walked down the volcanic rock the rest of the way, falling frequently due to the fatigue in my legs.

I fully recognized my need for help on this climb. The trust and relationships built among team members saved my life. I was humbled as my unflappable team members reached out to help and did not leave me behind. Everyone, including me, did not allow the psychological state of this epic event overshadow what tasks needed to be done.

I was weak, dealing with altitude sickness, and experiencing equipment failure. I was in a vulnerable state and could have easily lost my life on this climb. Even with my previous experiences at high altitude, the rapid increase in altitude (e.g., sea level, Mexico City-7,000 feet, Puebla 8500 feet, and the hut system 14,000 feet) within a 24-hour period gave rise to the ill effects of altitude.

Errors in judgment, stubbornness, and failure to ask for help are common examples of people in any leadership position. The pitfalls of determination can be dangerous. Stubbornness takes over and judgment takes a back seat.

Knowledge, skills, and experience are essential in developing good judgment. If one does not learn from past mishaps with correction, good judgment, a key component to leadership, never occurs.

Pico de Orizaba

On the summit of Pico de Orizaba

Reflective Questions

1. On a scale from one to ten, how easy is it for you to ask for help?

2. How important is TEAM in the success of your business and experiences? Is a shared purpose critical in selecting your TEAM?

3. How do you use your past experiences to guide you in future decisions?

6

ASSUMPTIONS ON
MT. KILIMANJARO

When I was a child in the 1960's, I played a vintage African animal lotto bingo game on Saturday evening TV. I was fascinated by the big animals shown on the show and hoped I would have three African animals in a row to win something. I was also a fan of watching the TV show *Tarzan* at that time.

By the time I got to graduate school in 1982, Toto was a famous rock band who recorded the song "Africa." I loved the music and romanticized going there someday to see the big game animals and climb Mt. Kilimanjaro. In 1996, nearly fifteen years later, the opportunity was before me.

I wrote a grant for the International Studies Program at Longwood College/University in 1996. The grant was to explore Kenya, Tanzania, and do reconnaissance in Ghana to investigate Longwood's exchange opportunities, for both faculty and students. I turned forty that year and wanted to celebrate this milestone and the next decade by starting off with a challenging physical feat. I received some grant monies to offset the cost of going to Africa, which helped in my pursuit.

I traveled alone and met Eric in Nairobi, one of the guys I climbed with in Mexico two years earlier. We both successfully reached Mt. Kilimanjaro's summit at 5:30 am on June 12, 1996. As with many of my adventures, I wanted to share this experience with students by providing an adventure trip to Africa to climb Mt. Kilimanjaro and go on a Serengeti Safari.

Bringing value and experience to others is core to leadership.

The following year, I began planning my first international trip offered to students and people in the community where I lived and worked at Longwood College. The two best seasons to climb Mt. Kilimanjaro are January to March and June to October.

I decided to offer a trip over the new year in 1997/1998. Four students from Longwood, the chief of police, a faculty member, a man who worked with the Sierra Club, and a highly regarded and loved physician from Farmville comprised the group.

In February the pre-trip planning and preparations began. I presented the members the following: the trip itinerary, an information sheet outlining the dangers of high altitude, a memorandum of understanding and liability form, and a suggested exercise regime to motivate members to be in good physical condition for the trip. Although Harold, the physician on the trip, was a smoker, he planned to quit as we both knew smoking would compromise his well-being as we moved up in altitude. The adventure of climbing Mt. Kilimanjaro was a desire of his and his enthusiasm was evident.

His secretary said he had quit smoking and was exercising on a Nordic machine to get in shape. I was pleased to hear this. There was no "rule" against smoking, and I certainly didn't feel it was my place to tell a man older than I and a highly respected physician that he could not go on the trip.

As we were waiting for our flight to Nairobi, Kenya at the Washington Dulles airport, Harold pulled out some thin cigars and began smoking them. I quickly recognized that Harold had a will and mind of his own. He operated on his time and conducted himself in his way. I wondered if his military background coupled with his power of making life and death decisions kept him from fully participating as a "student" on the trip.

As a female leader, 12 years his junior, I wasn't convinced I had his support to guide and make calls for him on the trip. I found myself creating beliefs about what he might be thinking based on his behaviors and reactions.

Creating wrong beliefs can dismantle one's strength as a leader.

Harold and I were early morning risers, so we shared a few breakfasts together in Nairobi and talked about his thoughts for retiring. He talked about some physical issues regarding the steadiness of his hands. He was thinking about what he may do and how difficult it would be for him to have to leave the profession. He loved his job as a Physician.

While in Nairobi we toured some of the cultural sites for two days and then headed to Arusha, Tanzania about a 6-hour drive. Arusha is considered the gateway to Mt. Kilimanjaro and Moshi was the closest town to the base of the mountain. We met our guides at the Capricorn Hotel, had a good dinner, and left the next morning to begin the Marangu route at 6,000 feet. We signed in at the park entrance and met our porters and trekking guides. We arrived at the Mandara Hut at 9,000 feet by 2:30 in the afternoon.

Because it was New Year's Eve, there were people staying at the Mandara hut who were celebrating the new year after midnight while our group tried to rest for the next day's trek. Regardless, it was exciting to bring in the New Year on Mt. Kilimanjaro.

We had awakened to the new year, 1998. The weather was a bit overcast and the temperature was dropping the higher we climbed in altitude. The group seemed to be doing ok as they adjusted to altitude. Rob's knee was bothering him, and Jen's ankle was giving her some problems. But overall the group was up to hiking and still excited about moving up the mountain.

The next hut system was called Horombo Hut at 12,000 feet. It took about 5.5 hours to arrive at the hut. People continued feeling the impacts of altitude such as walking slowly, breathing deeply, feeling tired, etc.

I encouraged everyone to continue drinking water, at least a gallon a day. We would raise our Nalgene bottles in a toast at the tables at dinner time. Grades were given for how much water they were drinking. An 'A' was given to those who drank a gallon and subsequent B's and C's under that. Harold generally did not sit with the group when we talked about the plan for the next day and shared how everyone was doing and feeling. He didn't "appear" interested in the debriefs or discussions, although he did tell me separately that he was listening even though it appeared he was not.

Actions are not always what they appear to be.

January 2nd, 1998 took us to Kibo hut at 15,500 feet, the last hut system before making the push to the summit. The group was now struggling. Heart rates were higher than normal, people did not feel their best due to altitude, some headaches, and generally feeling the greater impacts of altitude. One student returned to the lower hut system with a porter and the others made it to Kibo.

The next morning, Harold, Jimmy, and Meredith returned to the lower hut at 12,000 feet. They had climbed as high as they wanted. Stephen, Steve, D.R., Rob, and I left for the summit at 12:30 am. When we reached about 17,000 feet, the wind was blowing snow around in a blizzard-like fashion. The snows of Kilimanjaro are a real thing. The weather was so different from when I climbed the mountain in June of 1996.

Rob and Stephen made it to nearly 17,000 feet and decided to return to the Kibo hut with a guide and then on to Horombo Hut. The two male students (D.R. and Steve) and I continued up the mountain. We were a bit spread out but we each had a guide to ensure our safety.

We made it to Gillman's point, the crater rim at 19,000 feet.

It was another 300 feet to reach the summit of Mt. Kilimanjaro, but the snow was almost hip deep, and the guides said it was unsafe. We returned via a scree/talus slope (an accumulation of loose small rocks), using the gravity of the moving rocks to get us back to Kibo hut much faster.

On arriving back to Horombo Hut after Kibo, the first thing I noticed was Harold sitting outside on the steps to his hut smoking a cigarette. I said, "Harold, what are you doing?" He didn't seem concerned, he just wanted to have a cigarette. Again, he didn't seem to pay much attention to my directions or alter his behavior. He appeared fine, nothing dramatic.

No one else in his hut, including Harold, indicated anything different so I continued to let him do what he wished. Besides, we were heading back down to 6,000 feet the very next day and we would all feel much better.

The next morning was a different story. Harold said, "Get me off this fuckin' mountain." This was a very different disposition from the evening before. He had difficulty walking and his vision was a bit blurred. There were porters on either side of him to assist him walking down the trail. Harold apologized several times for his condition which was a role reversal for him. As a physician, he was trained to take care of others. When we had a radio signal, we called for an ambulance which met us halfway between the Mandara huts and Marangu gate.

Harold, Jen, I, and the porters all rode in the ambulance. The road was nearly unnavigable with huge rocks, mud ruts left from the rainy season, and big drop offs. It was quite the bumpy ride to say the least.

We intended to go straight to the hospital in Moshi. Harold and I had three different dialogue exchanges in the vehicle.

He first said:
"Yes, I think I should go to the hospital."

His second comment was:
"I think I'm feeling better, and I don't think I need to go."

My response was:
"For peace of mind, I want you to go to the hospital. I am responsible for you."

Harold replied,
"I release you from responsibility. I'm a big boy."

Then there was a pause, and I said,
"Let's go to the hospital."

He replied by saying,
"Okay."

After a few more minutes Harold said,
"I'm not going to the hospital."

He then quoted a statistic from an article he brought with him on the trip about AIDS contracted in hospitals. He was concerned about the medical staff giving him a transfusion.

He said,
"I'm feeling better and I'm not going to the hospital."

I said,

"Okay, as long as you promise me that you will drink water and hydrate yourself."

I allowed Harold to take the leadership away from me.

Harold was a loved man and a master of his trade. He was bold, humorous, somewhat sarcastic, witty, very stubborn, AND, he was a physician. I *assumed* he knew about the human body, and I had a firm belief that he and all the others took the information I gave them about the effects of altitude seriously.

Once back at the Capricorn Hotel, Harold asked to have his own room. He had been rooming with Stephen at the hotels and in the huts, so it was an awkward request. But I complied.

Again, I assumed that with a needed shower, hydrating, and a good night's rest, he would be ok and ready to go the following day. I trusted he would be drinking water and taking care of himself. He tried calling his wife, but the phones were not working that evening.

I was always the first up in the morning, and I immediately went to Harold's room. He was up too! We sat on his bed, talking about how he was doing and feeling. He said he felt a bit better, but he wasn't going on the Safari. He said,

"You all go and have a good time, and I'll either meet you back here or meet you in Nairobi."

Again, his matter-of-fact tone and his "in charge" disposition lured me to *assume* he would be fine. The Capricorn Hotel manager said he would look in on him while we were away. Once again, he verbalized that he was a "big boy."

Making assumptions can be dangerous.

After breakfast and before the group set out on Safari, I asked each of them to go to Harold's room to say good-bye. Although we had only been together for less than a week, he was a member of the group, and everyone really enjoyed him. There is something unique and memorable about sharing time with others on an outdoor adventure and experiencing a challenge together.

Harold died the evening of January 5th, the day we departed for safari. However, no one could reach us by phone, so we didn't know until we returned to the Capricorn Hotel four days later. "WHAT?" I was stunned. "How could that be?" The death report indicated he died of pulmonary edema and severe dehydration causing kidney failure.

I was the leader, the woman "in charge," the one taking care of the group. I was broken as a leader. I reviewed what went wrong over and over for the next ten years. What signs did I miss? I had been at high altitudes many times previously, observed others with altitude sickness and had experienced my own altitude sickness. The signs and symptoms did not point to the degree that there was danger in losing a life. Questions I asked myself:

- Would I have taken care of him differently if he were a student?

- If he were another student and not Harold would I have left him alone at the hotel?

- Because he was a physician, had I assumed he knew more than he really did?

- If he were not a bold and strong male, would I have been more forceful and direct with him as the leader in monitoring his behaviors throughout the trip?

I led people on successful wilderness trips and expeditions for nearly 20 years at this point. I was an instructor at two renowned wilderness leadership organizations: Wilderness Education Association (WEA) and the National Outdoor Leadership School (NOLS), and lead college students on multiple adventure trips. I experienced minor injuries and a few non-life-threatening evacuations, but this experience was far beyond anything I previously encountered. Losing a member of a group I was responsible for in a foreign country stretched my leadership experience and responsibility.

I was navigating in the dark and using my best knowledge and human understanding to make decisions about the group: the logistics of returning the body to the United States and deciding to continue or end the trip. I was also concerned for the well-being of the group members. The despair surrounding the group impacted my leadership effectiveness. I was a failure; I didn't bring everyone back from the trip.

The monumental lessons learned from this trip were:

- The perils in allowing someone to take the leadership away from me.

- The limitations of being the only leader responsible for the group.

- The ability to set consistent boundaries.

- Ensuring I hold everyone to the same standard regardless of gender, age, disposition, or circumstances.

- The danger in making assumptions about others' knowledge, skills, and abilities.

Significant judgments were gained leading me to make intentional changes in my future leadership decisions and actions. The one constant was the unflappable demonstration of how I handled the events of this trip. Although I experienced turmoil inside, I worked pragmatically with the "authorities," and those group members who were returning to the U.S. with Harold's body. I encouraged students to share their thoughts and feelings.

The events and the altered dynamics of the group impacted my own psychological well-being. The focus on my students and their welfare, contributed to my ability to keep leading. Having never been down this road before, I relied on my ability to remain outwardly calm in this stormy situation.

Longwood Group at Horombo Hut

Mt. Kilimanjaro is in the background

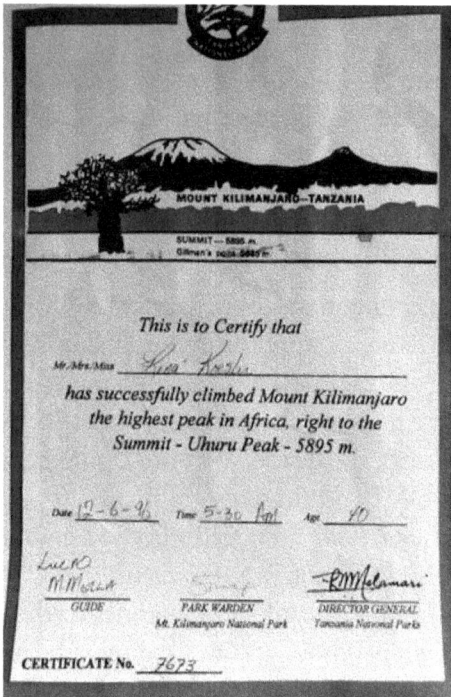

Certificate of Completion - 1996

**On my way to the summit of
Mt. Kilimanjaro - 1996**

Reflective Questions

1. When have you made assumptions about another person or a situation? What were the results of those assumptions?

2. When was there a time when you altered your leadership behavior based upon a person's age, gender, disposition, or behavior?

3. What do you think is the most important leadership skill to demonstrate in a crisis?

7

THE ALLURE OF
MT. EVEREST

Harold's death continued to be fresh on my mind as I set out to travel alone to Nepal a month later, February 1998. I was on a sabbatical leave from Longwood College. My sabbatical research involved investigating the environmental degradation of the more popular trekking routes in Nepal.

There was so much written about the trash at Mt. Everest Base Camp (EBC). I was interested in learning how the Nepalese government was pursuing greater protection at EBC and the cleanup of other highly visited areas.

To see Mt. Everest was a long-awaited desire of mine. I wanted to see the highest mountain in the world, meet the Sherpa culture, and better understand the stories and articles written about climbing Mt. Everest.

I communicated with my trekking guide Pemba, by email and fax since there was no internet access yet. He greeted me at the Kathmandu airport with a *Khata*, a scarf given to arriving guests symbolizing a welcome to Nepal. I arrived in late February and was about to begin my next adventure.

Pemba took good care of me as I spent nearly two months in Nepal. I trekked to EBC and traveled to the Pokhara area in Nepal to trek to the Annapurna Base Camp (ABC). I spent time meeting with Nepalese agencies and officials to learn about what environmental projects were in progress to protect these beautiful landscapes.

The seven weeks that I spent traveling in Nepal was not only productive but revitalizing and rewarding. Upon returning to the United States, I had a renewed belief in myself and the energy returned to continue sharing adventures and cultures with student groups. I wanted to prove to myself, more than anyone, that I could lead a group safely and enjoyably on an international adventure.

I spent the following academic year educating and building a group to return to Nepal. I conducted informational classes about the country and culture, meeting regularly, and had a few preparatory hikes in the Blue Ridge Mountains. I put even more emphasis and attention on the dangers involved in trekking at altitude.

It was an eclectic group: four Longwood students, the chief of police at Longwood who had been with me on the Mt. Kilimanjaro trip, a friend from graduate school, and a Longwood professor.

This was quite an adventure for everyone. Recognizing that they would be away from friends, family and the American way of life for five weeks created both excitement and nervousness. We departed after academic finals week in early May and returned mid June.

The group worked well together. They were conscientious about hydrating and supporting each other through the physical challenges along the way. They also enjoyed learning about the Sherpa culture, eating the traditional foods, and appreciating the enormity of the Himalayan mountains.

After eight days of trekking from one village to the next and slowly acclimatizing, we arrived at the last village (Gorak Shep) at 17,000 ft. before going to EBC. Everyone was taking Diamox which helped in reducing the impacts of altitude sickness but also created a raspy dry cough the higher we went.

We moved slowly as we approached EBC. Seeing the expedition tents scattered about the boulder field and viewing the Khumbu icefall up close was both fascinating and breath taking, respectively. We took a group photo and returned to Gorak Shep for a rest in preparation for climbing Kala Patthar the following day.

Most of the group members climbed Kala Patthar (18,500 feet), presenting a spectacular view of Mt. Everest, Pumori, Ama Dablam and the Khumbu icefall. Heather, one of the students, stayed behind because she was not feeling well. When the group returned from the climb, Heather had thrown up, so the group immediately descended to Lobuche at 16,000 feet.

We spent the night there, but Heather was now experiencing breathing difficulties. I instructed the group to stay behind with a porter. We would meet them later in the day while I traveled with Heather.

The porters carried Heather down 3,000 feet to Tukla and then on to Tengboche at 12,600 feet. They were moving fast, and I traveled with lightning speed to keep up with them. Once the group caught up with us much later in Tengboche, Heather was feeling better.

She was now eating and getting her sense of humor back. From Tengboche, we continued our trek back to Lukla at 9,000 feet. In 36 hours, Heather was back to her old self.

The trip ended in a full celebration with the porters, guides, and the entire group dancing and singing the night away. Everyone who was on the trip returned home safe and well. It was the leadership confirmation I needed. It boosted my conviction knowing I could lead a group safely and enjoyably on an international adventure trip.

I continued to lead other student groups on international trips in the future, returning to Africa and Nepal, Chile (Patagonia) and Ireland.

When you know better, you do better.

The above quote by Maya Angelou was a powerful message to me. The death of Harold was tragic and unfortunate. However, it was on the Africa trip where my leadership grew in leaps and bounds from the events that I encountered. It is not what you KNOW but what you DO with that knowledge. Judgment is often gained from previous errors if you intentionally make the improved changes in the future.

Longwood Group at the IAD Airport

Longwood Group at Mt. Everest Base Camp – 1999

Mt. Everest and the Khumbu Icefall

On the summit of Mt. Kala Patthar
(18,500 ft.) 1998

Reflective Questions

1. How important is it to act quickly in an emergency?

2. Was there a time when a mistake, a failure, or a bad experience created more insight and growth than if it were a successful experience?

3. How valuable is reflection in the process of gaining judgment to take with you in future experiences?

4. What benefits have you gained in reflection?

8

CLIMBING THE GRAND TETON

I have been to Wyoming nearly every summer since my first introduction in 1977. My season as a rafting guide on the Salmon River in Idaho ended the summer of 1987. Before returning to work at Longwood College in Virginia, I decided to climb the Grand Teton. It was time to climb the mountain I had looked up to for ten years.

I met my friend Barb in Jackson, and off we went with ropes, harnesses, and hardware. We backpacked up to Garnett Canyon in Grand Teton National Park and camped overnight. We started early the next morning heading up to the lower saddle (the lowest point between two high points), then the upper saddle and across the ledge called *Wall Street*. This marks the approach to begin roping up and start the technical part of the climb.

It was an intermediate climb, rated at 5.7 (climbing scale) and involved six technical pitches (6-150 ft. rope lengths) to the top. No helmet and no protection, other than a belay (a person taking up slack or feeding rope to the climber as they climb) as we climbed to the next pitch.

It wasn't uncommon at this time to see climbers without a helmet. The weather was perfect, the climb was challenging, mostly due to the exposure, the rappel to descend was straight-forward, and the reward for climbing the Grand Teton was extremely gratifying.

In 2014 I had another yearning to climb the Grand Teton. I was nearly 30 years older but no less enthusiastic about making the climb with three of my good friends and former students.

Cameron, my former student, was living in Wyoming, working at the National Outdoor Leadership School (NOLS) and climbing daily. When asked, he gladly accepted the opportunity to be our climbing guide on the Grand Teton.

As noted earlier, the climb is a technical six pitch, moderate 5.7 grade climb (from a scale of 5.1-5.15). The greatest challenge is the exposure as we moved up the various pitches. This time we wore helmets, had lead climbing hardware, climbing shoes, and a couple of ropes.

As we had done in 1987, we camped in Garnett Canyon and got up early to get to the lower saddle by sunrise. Except, on this morning, it was overcast and very few people on the mountain. Upon reaching the upper saddle, the look of the weather to the west toward the Idaho side made us stop and discuss our next moves. We asked ourselves several questions:

- Do you think the pending rainstorm will hold until we get to the top?

- How is everyone feeling?

- How prepared are we as a team (weather, gear, skill, and endurance)?

- Does anyone have doubts or want to return?

In other words, we are either all in or we go back to our basecamp. Since Cameron and I had lived in Wyoming, we had a greater sense about Wyoming weather than the other members coming from Virginia. After a healthy discussion, we collectively decided to go for it. We proceeded along Wall Street and on to our first pitch.

The weather held through all six pitches until we reached the top. There were no views from the top since a thick fog had set in. After taking photos of our summit accomplishment, we proceeded to find the rappel anchor to begin our descent.

In good weather, it takes two rappels to get to the place where we can safely walk or climb down towards the rocky trail back to our camp. However, the fog turned into a consistent drizzle which intensified our focus on safety. Instead of two rappels, we set up four rappels to increase the safety and reduce the possibility of errors due to slick, wet rocks.

We started at 3:30 am and returned by 4:00 pm. By the time we reached our base camp, the rain stopped, but the dampness and cold temperatures lingered. We were chilled but safe and sound. We ate a warm, hearty dinner and were in the tents by 7:00 pm.

It is precisely these situations that warrant a good deal of reflection. There is great value to tap into your judgment under circumstances that are not clear and easily navigable. Under these conditions, it gives rise for additional attention and uncovering psychological resources that have been developed over years of being in the mountains in uncertain situations.

Since all of us on the trip had been outdoor adventure leaders, we agreed we would have returned to base camp if we were leading students. Our responsibility for the group's safety would have been paramount. However, given our care and knowledge of each other, knowing something about each person's ability, and trusting others' judgments and skills gave us the reassurance that we could do this as a team.

Leadership is developed through direct experience, in stepping out and taking risks, in the decision-making process, in good preparation, and trusting the skills and abilities of others to foster the TEAM attitude. Leadership is instilling confidence in others and developing a team mindset. Good judgment is a product of skills, knowledge, and experience. It is the ability to step forward or step away when one of these three factors is compromised.

Me and Barb on the top of Grand Teton – 1987

Nearing the summit of the Grand Teton – 1987

Dan, me, and Cameron
The summit of the Grand Teton – 2014

Reflective Questions

1. Why is communication and respect for others important in developing a team?

2. How have previous leadership experiences improved your judgment and decision-making abilities?

3. Do you challenge yourself to learn and grow outside of your leadership responsibilities? How do you use those experiences to strengthen your skills and confidence as a leader?

9

SOLO TO MT. WHITNEY

I am a huge John Muir fan. I talked a lot about him in the Environmental Education course I taught at Longwood University. He was a significant contributor to the conservation movement and in wilderness protection in the late 1800's and early 1900's.

I was drawn to know more about him, his life, and his wilderness wanderings. His writing and connection to God in nature resonates with my spiritual core. Like John Muir, I feel closest to God when I am in nature. The majesty, the beauty, the natural wonders that are everywhere awaken my relationship to something bigger and more powerful than me.

I finally had the opportunity to visit Yosemite National Park in 2009. John Muir was a force in establishing the area as a national park in 1890. I visited many John Muir landmarks while I was there: Muir Woods, his California home, Hetch Hetchy, and the John Muir Trail

(JMT) in Yosemite National Park. While hiking in the park with my friend Barb, we met three young men about to embark on the JMT. Their enthusiasm unleashed my desire to hike the 211-mile trail.

The following year, Barb and I decided to hike the second half of the JMT, from Bishop Pass to Mt. Whitney. It was glorious! The beauty of the Sierra mountains, the abundance of wildflowers, and the challenge of the many mountain passes and stream crossings gave rise to much joy and inspiration for the wilderness experience.

Climbing Mt. Whitney, the highest peak in the lower 48 states, was exceptional. I wondered how many times John Muir climbed this peak and looked out over the breathtaking views of the Sierra.

In 2012, I returned to Yosemite and hiked the first half of the JMT to Bishop Pass, this time by myself. I longed for a solo trip in the wilderness for an extended period. The Sierra mountains never disappoint. I discovered the comfort of being in the wilderness alone with no communication with the outside world, and where decisions are reduced to about five a day.

- Where will I camp?

- What will I eat?

- How do I feel?

- Where is the next water stop?

- Do I have the right gear?

Since there were no influences from the civilized world, I relied entirely on myself and my faith throughout the experience. I got "misplaced" once as I completely missed a trail junction which continued on the other side of a stream.

I spent a few hours walking up and down and around the wrong trail saying to myself "this is not the right trail as it should be on the other side of the stream." I finally discovered the continuation of the correct trail on the far side of the stream and off I went shaking my head saying, "how in the world did I miss that trail?"

I trusted my navigational skills and used my faith to remain unflappable and directed. I suffered some blisters, lost five pounds, got a hole in my sleeping pad the last two nights, endured a loud thunder and lightning storm and didn't want the adventure to end when I got to the South Lakes trailhead near Bishop ten days later.

I retired from Longwood University in 2018 and decided to return to the JMT in September, starting at Tuolumne Meadows and hiking to Whitney Portal. Each time I traveled the JMT trail, my purpose for doing so was different. Hiking the 189 miles was a retirement present to myself.

This would be the longest time I had spent alone on a wilderness trek. The wilderness was the perfect choice for me to reflect on my career and consider the transition to the next phase of my life. Nature has always symbolized a place for peace, clarity, and even enlightenment.

I yearned for the time to be alone again. It allowed me the opportunity to lead myself, test and recognize my resourcefulness, honor the person I had become, and develop thoughts and visions about where I want to go to continue living out my mission. Once again, I chose to eliminate all communication with family, friends, and social media except for two random email messages delivered from my SPOT (a GPS tracking device that sends messages) that delivered this message: "All is well, wish you were here."

I spent weeks planning my meals, determined my food supply locations, poured over maps, designed my itinerary, and reduced the amount of weight in my pack without compromising my comfort and safety. Breaking off the handle of my toothbrush, determining which shirt weighed less, and weighing every item helped me to discern my material "needs" from luxury "wants."

Encountering others along the trail fully added to my wilderness experience. Everyone was on their own personal journey and chose the wilderness to enlighten their lives in some way. I saw many more women trekking alone than I had on previous JMT trips.

This was a good sign. I appreciated that more women, like myself, were intentionally seeking opportunities to support their independence and tap into the strength and courage uncovered and enhanced on a solo wilderness experience. As on most trips, I kept a journal of thoughts, reflections, and daily encounters.

On day sixteen, September 13th, I headed toward Mt. Whitney. I had plans to camp above Guitar Lake near the base of Mt. Whitney. But given the ice build-up along the trail, hiking early the next morning would only make those conditions worse and compromise my safety along the trail in the dark. I fought the wind and the altitude all the way to the summit, alone.

The wind was incredibly forceful, enough to blow an average-sized person off their feet on uneven rocky terrain. The views were stunning, but I spent more time trying to stay upright. I signed the registry and headed down the 99 switchbacks from 14,500 feet to 9,000 feet.

It ended up being an 18-mile day and I was beat. Arriving at Whitney Portal the next morning was euphoric. I celebrated by ordering a huge breakfast of scrambled eggs, two large pancakes, bacon, and tea.

I was pleasantly full, considering my diet the past 17 days consisted mostly of freeze-dried dinners, oatmeal, tortillas, peanut butter, mini-sausages, energy bars, beef jerky and hard candy for a quick snack "pick me up" along the trail. My mind and outlook were clearer, my body was strong, I was 10 pounds lighter, and I had no desire to check my phone for communication or to hear the latest news. I was completely content with what I had experienced and the "unflappable" spirit that followed.

I spent the days on the trail leading myself in mind, body, and spirit. I was renewed, refreshed, and eager to step into the next unknown phase of my life. I was excited and rejuvenated to launch the next chapter. I've never been wrong or mislead before when I followed my God-given spirit to which I pay attention. My faith is a vital component to leading. It is the foundation to who I am, where I go and the decisions I make.

I didn't have a clear vision, but I knew at my core that I was not done climbing mountains and reaching summits. I wanted to continue moving toward my mission:

Seeking inspiration to ignite the inspiration in others.

Leadership requires time alone to bring clarity and direction to future steps. I would not have capitalized on the depth and insight I gained if I had been with other people on the trip.

Mt. Whitney

On the summit of Mt. Whitney

Reflective Questions

1. When was the last time you spent time alone, without distractions, to reflect on your present and future outlook?

2. Under what circumstances and conditions do you feel the greatest worth and resourcefulness?

3. What has been your greatest accomplishment and why?

10

CLIMBING ISLAND PEAK: TWENTY YEARS IN THE MAKING

Island Peak was pointed out to me on my first visit to Nepal in 1998. I distinctly recall Pemba, my Nepalese trekking guide, telling me, "People climb that mountain, and you have the strength and ability to climb that mountain too."

The perfectly symmetrical shape of the mountain reminded me of Mt. Rainier in Washington State, a mountain I climbed in 1995. I couldn't stop thinking about how striking it looked, how beautiful it was and how it was within my abilities, according to Pemba.

With the subsequent four trips to Nepal, I thought about the mountain and the initial conversation I had with Pemba. I thought my desire to climb the mountain would go away but it kept creeping into my subconscious like a butterfly that lands on my shoulder and then flutters away only to return.

I eventually gave in saying "If I am going to do this mountain, I need to do it now." In 2019, at sixty-three and a half years old, and twenty years later, I made the decision to finally follow through with my desire.

Unlike my previous four visits to Nepal, I decided to do the climb in October instead of the previous April/May time period. It was also a popular trekking season and I could make some comparisons between the two seasons.

The time seemed to be right as I was psychologically and physically prepared for this climb. Since moving to Colorado after retiring from Longwood University in 2018, I now had the flexibility. Living in Colorado really helped prepare me for the altitude and getting my trekking legs used to hiking daily.

I learned early on in my leadership career, that thoughtful planning and preparation builds belief and confidence as a leader.

I invited others who I thought would and could share this quest with me. Jennie (a former student) and Ken (my adventure friend with whom I climbed the Grand Teton) met me in Kathmandu to begin this adventure together. After a few days of touring Kathmandu, we flew to Lukla, a 45-minute flight to the Himalayan village that serves as the gateway to trekking to Mt. Everest.

For two weeks we trekked seven to eight miles daily, stopping for lunch and spending our nights in Tea Houses, Sherpa housing scattered along the main trekking route to Everest Base Camp (EBC). We sandwiched in a few acclimatization days where we spent a few nights in one place to better prepare us to move up in altitude.

We trekked our way to EBC (17,600 feet.) followed by the climb of Mt. Kala Patthar (18,500 feet). Standing at the top and taking in the 360-degree vastness of Mt. Everest and the Khumbu icefall inspired me and enlivened all my senses. Although I had done these treks before, I knew the worth of getting to higher altitude in preparation for reaching the 20,300-foot Island Peak summit.

We were now headed to the base camp of Island Peak (16,200 feet). As we trekked to the village of Dingboche and on to Chukung, the view of Island Peak was clear and directly in front of us.

The time was finally here. I was feeling strong and found I was beginning to mentally prepare for the climb of Island Peak. Quieting my spirit, focusing on my next steps, paying extra attention to how I was feeling, and adding words of strength and success to my self-talk added to my confidence. The anticipation and the excitement were real and bound together.

Ken was not feeling well when we awakened at midnight on October 15th. In consultation with our trekking guide, we decided it was best he stay behind and perhaps move to a lower altitude while Jennie, me, and our climbing guide began the climb up, leaving at 1:00am. We had a full moon to guide our way. Not once did we need our headlamps as the bright moon illuminated the deep dark sky around us.

The climb to higher altitude was daunting. I quickly realized that this trek was harder and steeper than I had anticipated. Although I was physically prepared, I felt underprepared and was slower than Jennie and our guide. The thought of turning back never entered my mind as I was determined to keep putting one foot in front of the other. I felt the need for more oxygen and felt the expansion of my lungs the higher we got.

By the time we reached the glacier, it was nearly sunrise. Seeing the light and how the sunrise was coloring the peaks around us, brightened my spirit. We ate a snack, put our plastic boots and crampons on, snapped on our helmets and grabbed our ice axes. We clipped our carabiners into our harnesses and moved across the glacier toward the mountain connected as a team of three by rope.

The progress we made toward the summit gave me the motivation to continue. No time to think, no time to question, no time to doubt. Although the altitude was testing my strength and deepening my breathing, my spirit was soaring. I was closer than I had ever been to reaching Island Peak and that desire kept me moving.

There is strength and power in desire.

Once we reached the base of Island Peak, we could see people climbing up the headwall on a fixed rope using jumars, a spring-loaded cam device that tightens around the rope when weight is applied on the ascent. Our guide said it was another three hours to the top. I couldn't believe it as we could now see the top. The saying "short to the eye, long to the feet" made perfect sense at this stage.

I wondered and wondered again, what do I have in me to make this final push? A push was an understatement as it took every ounce of will I had to slide the jumar along the rope and pull up on the locked jumar to make the next step. The altitude and the lack of oxygen made me feel as if I had no prior physical preparation.

It's intimidating to know that my strength at 20,000 feet feels like I just ran two marathons back-to-back. The oxygen is simply not running through my body as efficiently as it is at lower altitudes. The strength I felt at 8,000 ft or even 14,000 feet is dramatically reduced at 20,000 feet.

Take three steps, pull, rest, and breathe. Take another three steps, pull, rest, and breathe. This full body workout continued as I repeated this process over and over and over again. Nearly three hours later, we were there. I bent over at the waist and laid on the summit, with my crampons below me. One more pull up and I stood at the top. The first words I said were: This is the hardest thing I've ever done." Then I said, "Thank you, Lord."

The windless summit was very small, probably the smallest summit I had ever stood on. There were three others from Ukraine who had just summited so adding our group of three made for very little room to move about. The 360-degree views of the towering snow-white mountain peaks up against a sapphire sky were beyond words that could not be found in a dictionary. This was an extraordinary moment, and a feeling of AWE I had never experienced to this depth.

I was thrilled to have reached a summit and a desire that I longed over for 20 years. I had never reached that level of determination in my life and was beyond proud to discover the *WILL* I didn't know I had.

I felt comfortable and strong descending the summit as I relied on my empowered energy to rappel down the 330-foot headwall of the mountain, back across the glacier, to the rock section, and return to base camp. One does not know their determination and will until it is tested. After a 16-hour day, I was spent, but had enough energy to reward myself with a pizza at our tea house in Chukung.

This was yet another mountain that inspired me to put one foot in front of the other. The biggest battle was asking myself "what is this worth to me?" "How important is this for me?" "What would I do if I had to turn around?" The climb represented every fiber of who I am–the power in desire to keep moving. It translates to all areas of my life where preparation, risk, grit, determination, follow through, and will speak volumes on the road to living a significant and meaningful life.

I had a journey where a destination was involved. But it was in the journey that prepared me to reach the summit. In hindsight, I needed the 20-year journey. Visiting Nepal over the years, discerning the value and importance this climb had for me, and the timing and place of my psychological and physical preparation was key.

This climb represented one more summit reached that inspired me to continue following through with my life's mission. This climb, once again, confirmed the power in desire, regardless of age, gender, disability, or any other imagined limiting belief. Desire and passion are real and can take you places you never thought you would go. This climb reignited my purpose and narrowed my focus with intention and determination to launch my own coaching business. Within two months I wrote my first book and expanded my desire to help others reach the metaphorical summits in their own life.

Our climbing guide, me, and Jennie Island Peak

Me, Ken, and Jennie. On our way to Island Peak

Island Peak

Reflective Questions

1. What summit or goal have you been longing for but have yet to reach it?

2. Do you understand the value of knowing your will and determination? What will give you a greater understanding of this for you?

3. How important is planning and preparation to your success in leadership and confidence?

Conclusion

Although I didn't know what the word *unflappable* meant in 1981, I learned the enormous value it had on me and other leaders in decision making, emergencies, and setting the tone for their team, followers, and/or employees.

Some people are wired more naturally with an unflappable disposition. I don't think I recognized I was one of them until someone brought it to my attention. However, one can learn to be unflappable by:

- Knowing who you are: The leader's best friend.

- Accumulating knowledge, skills, and experience.

- Making time for good planning and preparation.

- Acquiring experience in new, novel, and unknown situations.

- Developing judgment gained from previous experiences.

- Having faith in something bigger and mightier than yourself.

Accepting the risks, experiencing the unpredictable weather, and enduring the physical and mental stamina to climb mountains has added to my unflappable responses. All of these factors boost confidence and more readily unleash calm and unflappable character that consistently benefits leaders over time.

I bundled together the characteristics I believe foster good leadership in any line of work, in any situation, or in any relationship-building encounter you have:

1. **Influence without character is dead-end leadership**
   Trust in self and others, honesty, integrity, follow through, and consistency speak volumes in demonstrating good character-based leadership.

2. **Demonstrating unselfishness and bringing value to others**
   As a leader you are number two and your students, employees, customers, and others who follow you are number one. Seeking *significance* in leadership (bringing value to others) multiplies much farther than seeking *success* (your accomplishments) in leadership.

3. **Consistency**
   Consistency in leadership, regardless of the situation, can encourage ease, trust, and approachability with your students, participants, employees, and customers.

4. The hardest person to lead is yourself

There is strength and power in keeping the hinges oiled on the door to personal development. Self-development throughout life can create stronger relationships and connections with others – a most valuable factor in leading successfully.

5. Get up, show up, and be on time

These simple tasks require no training, credentials, or additional education. They speak volumes to who you are and provide hints to how you operate in other areas of your life.

6. Ask for help

Reaching out to your participants/followers for assistance, skills, or talents you lack can lead to greater safety and enjoyment for all involved.

7. Judgment development

The value is in the learning process. Judgment is designed to learn from your experiences (positive or negative) to use and profit from those insights and judgments in future encounters.

8. Unflappable

Work at and practice the art of being unflappable during calamity, upset, surprises, and spontaneous occurrences. The unflappable ripple effect on those in your company creates the ease and calm needed to keep the group connected and working as a team.

9. Faith

Your faith can move mountains and your doubt can create them. Take time to meditate, pray, ask God and/or your higher power to bring clarity and then move to ignite your faith. Faith is not created unless you step out.

May you glean insight, enthusiasm,
and inspiration from these stories.

Better yet, I hope you consider these leadership components as you travel the road of living a life of significance
and influence in your work, family, and
personal relationships.

Reaching your own symbolic summits gives you the
fuel that powers your ambition and direction.

—Rená Koesler

About Rená

Rená is a Business Coach who is influenced and inspired by adventure. Although many of her summits are mountain summits, she has learned the strength, determination, and focus required in climbing mountains to help leaders and entrepreneurs grow their businesses and teams. There is value in taking risks, escaping the elusive comfort zone, and stepping out. She knows what it takes to pursue a challenge, a dream, or a goal. There is no growth without a willingness to go places where others may not go.

As a best-selling author, business coach and professional speaker, Rená Koesler meets and connects with people where they are in their life's journey. Mountain climber or not, old, or young, tall, or short, black, white, or brown, she is inspired by people who are on the trail to learn and grow. She fully recognizes that the summit is alluring and enticing. However,

...the learning is in the journey and the direction is found in your purpose.

Leadership development is a life-long process that makes you want to be better and do better. You must begin, you have to take risks, you have to step out, and you have to be intentional about bringing value to others as you lead.

Rená is a midwesterner at her core but was transformed by the western mountains many years ago. As a former professor of Outdoor and Environmental Education, she was inspired by her students to be better and do better. Rená found much education and delight in traveling the world and leading students on domestic and international adventures. She lives in Colorado where she continues to include the great outdoors to educate, inspire, and challenge others to move and grow.

A Note from Rená

I hope you traveled alongside me as I unfolded the various successes and mishaps in my leadership encounters. Leadership development is a process where there is no finish line to learning and growing. I would be delighted to hear how this book enlightened you or broadened your thoughts about leadership. I want to hear your stories too.

Send your emails or letters to:

Email: Rena@renakoesler.com
Website: www.renakoesler.com

If you enjoyed *UNFLAPPABLE: Leadership Lessons from Climbing Mountains*, you may also enjoy her first book, *Achieving Your Potential: 15 Empowering Steps to Reach Each Summit.*

Rená Koesler is THE professional speaker for your next event. Rená is an author, business coach and professional speaker. She engages and energizes her audiences so that participants are directly involved in the outcomes of the program. She leaves no one behind.

If you wish to know more about booking Rená for a keynote, coaching, or workshop, please contact her.